Woman as Created by God

Woman

as Created by God

Cheryl Harris

Table of Contents

Table of Contents

Preface

As Believers, we should take the Bible seriously. When a contradiction appears, we lack understanding. Repetitive numbers and stories are used to convey context. In Gods wisdom, the truth is hidden in parables to protect it. The gospel writer may leave a cue in the middle of verses that gives direction and clarity. In the middle of Ephesians Paul says, "This is a great mystery: but I speak concerning Christ and the church." Ephesians 5:32   This is the key to understanding that Paul leaves for us, the key that unlocks the truth in Ephesians and 1 Corinthians about the Woman. What Paul is really telling us is by far more beautiful and far reaching, as far as eternity, than any physical or literal translation strewn with contradiction. The journey through this book is based on the words of Paul and what we discover is the "fellowship of the mystery."

> And to make all *men* see what is the fellowship of the mystery, which from the beginning of the world hath been hid in God, who created all things by Jesus Christ
> **Ephesians 3:9**

One Natural Act

There is only one natural act in the world that produces another human life, a human being. Woman is the womb of mankind: the protector, comforter, and nourisher of life itself. A man and a woman are partners with God in the creation of new life. This is sacred and was always thought of as sacred until modern times. Today sexual intercourse seems to mean less than sharing a meal and has been purposely separated from its mystery and divine nature. All generative life results from a union of the masculine and feminine and this balance is woven into the fabric of creation.

This does not mean that a woman cannot be a woman or be fulfilled without having a baby or even wanting a baby, but only woman was created with the ability to give birth and nurse an infant. Every cell in our bodies, whether man or woman, is developed from conception according to our sexual design.

When we look at nature, we find cooperation

and balance. Although many would have you believe it is the opposite and opposing. A man and a woman are perfect complements, like two pieces of a puzzle looking for the adjoining puzzle piece. The puzzle pieces are not identical and do not all look alike. Rather, each piece ventures to find its corresponding match or chooses to stand alone.

Whether we are men or women is defined by nature and biology and begins the moment the sperm enters the egg. All eggs contain one X chromosome, while sperm contain either an X or a Y chromosome. Embryos with XY chromosomes develop male sex organs, while those with XX chromosomes develop female sex organs. The sperm determines a baby's sex.

Biology has always determined whether you are a man or a woman. What we choose to do with our lives is determined by our talents, passions, personalities, and character. Science has been able to manipulate the outward appearance of the human body with surgery, but science cannot reverse nine months of development by giving someone a fake breast or a fake penis or hormones.

Your sex is not determined by the clothes you take out of the closet and put on your body or by what your talents and hobbies are or by what you choose to do for a living or by intelligence or character. A man is a human being that is male and a woman is a human being that is female. Men and women are both fully human beings, both created in the image of God, each with a mind, body, and soul. Feminine and masculine are equal in significance and unique in attributes. Who you are is what you think, what you do, how you treat others, and how you walk through your day. What you are is a human being who is either male or female. "So God created man in his own image, in the image of God created he him; male and female created he them" Genesis 1:27.

God has very few commandments for mankind. None of the commandments say a man must be this or a woman must be that. God commands that we treat each other as we would want to be treated and love others as ourselves. To this one rule are added specific commandments that illustrate how we should interact with each other and how we should interact with God. These commandments are for our benefit and show us how to live in peace and harmony with each other so that our lives may be long, healthy, and prosperous. Western society has adopted the secular, or worldly, commandments, such as laws against murder, stealing, and false witness, because they reflect common sense and fairness that most people agree with and gravitate towards.

The following chapters will explore what Paul is telling us about the "woman", and we will discover on this journey through 1 Corinthians and Ephesians that Paul is sharing the "mystery of Christ."

Chapter 2

Allegory, Parable, and Similitude

Jesus spoke in parables to illustrate the truth and to protect the truth. Consider the time that Jesus lived in and how dangerous it was to challenge state and religious authority. Parables are often defined as an earthly story with a heavenly meaning. Unbelievers look at biblical stories and make fun of them and deride Christian beliefs because they don't perceive the meaning.

To those with eyes to see and ears to hear, the parables convey meaning. To those who wish to destroy the teachings of Jesus, the parable protects and covers the truth. Yet the biblical truths are not hidden from anyone who wishes to seek them out. Jesus explained the meanings of some of the parables to his disciples and the Bible defines itself. Before you can discern the truth, you must study the Word. This is the hidden wisdom of God to protect His plan from the powers of darkness. Believers glorify God by reflecting God's glory, and they do this by living lives that please God by understanding and living His Word.

Allegory

An allegorical interpretation is when a story becomes a symbol that stands for something else. The interpretation of allegory is not always readily clear, and a person or event may be used to stand for something larger or other than itself. In the following allegory, Jesus is the vine, and the believers are the branches.

> I am the true vine, and my Father is the husbandman.

> Every branch in me that beareth not fruit he taketh away: and every *branch* that beareth fruit, he purgeth it, that it may bring forth more fruit.

> Now ye are clean through the word which I have spoken unto you.

> Abide in me, and I in you. As the branch cannot bear fruit of itself, except it abide in the vine; no more can ye, except ye abide in me.

I am the vine, ye *are* the branches: He that abideth in me, and I in him, the same bringeth forth much fruit: for without me ye can do nothing.

If a man abide not in me, he is cast forth as a branch, and is withered; and men gather them, and cast *them* into the fire, and they are burned.

If ye abide in me, and my words abide in you, ye shall ask what ye will, and it shall be done unto you.

Herein is my father glorified, that ye bear much fruit; so shall ye be my disciples.

As the Father hath loved me, so have I loved you: continue ye in my love.
John 15:1-9

Parable

A parable is usually shorter than an allegory and designed to illustrate or teach a truth, heavenly concept, or moral story. Details in a parable can be used to help the story seem more realistic and hide the true meaning from the power of darkness. In Luke, the parable of the prodigal son is used to illustrate redemption and forgiveness.

And he answering said to *his* father, Lo, these many years do I serve thee, neither transgressed I at any time thy commandment: and yet thou never gavest me a kid, that I might make merry with my friends:

But as soon as this thy son was come, which hath devoured thy living with harlots, thou hast killed for him the fatted calf.

And he said unto him, Son, thou art ever with me, and all that I have is thine.

It was meet that we should make merry, and be glad: for this thy brother was dead, and is alive again; and was lost, and is found.
Luke 15:29-32

Similitude

Similitudes are used to illustrate complex theological ideas in a relatable and understandable manner through comparison. Jesus uses similitude to compare believers to salt and light in the following passages.

Ye are the salt of the earth: but if the salt has lost his savour, wherewith shall it be salted? It is thenceforth good for nothing, but to be cast out, and to be trodden under foot of men.

Ye are the light of the world. A city that is set on an hill cannot be hid.

Neither do men light a candle, and put it under a bushel, but on a candlestick; and it giveth light unto all that are in the house.

Let your light so shine before men, that they may see your good works, and glorify your Father which is in heaven.
Matthew 5:13-16

Allegory, parable, and similitude are important literary tools and understanding their use in the Bible is necessary to unlock the truth they are meant to convey. In Chapter 4 we are going to look closely at some of the most misunderstood words of Paul in the Bible.

Chapter 3

Meaning of Church

Church, congregation, and ecclesia are all names for the body of Christ, and the body of Christ includes all members from around the world who have faith in Jesus Christ risen. To have meaningful relationships and instruction, individual members of the body gather with fellow believers in local areas and local churches. Paul, in Ephesians and 1 Corinthians, describes the church as members of a single body, with different talents and gifts, who come together being stronger for the association, with one mind in the faith, love, and obedience to Jesus Christ our Lord, crucified for our sins, and our Savior and Redeemer.

> For as the body is one, and hath many members, and all the members of that one body, being many, are one body: so also *is* Christ.
> **1 Corinthians 12:12**

The body of Christ is often likened to a woman or

bride, to a virgin staying pure in her walk and faith while waiting for her husband and, if the church is in apostasy, likened to a harlot and a whore.

> For I am jealous over you with godly jealousy: for I have espoused you to one husband, that I may present *you* as a chaste virgin to Christ.
> **2 Corinthians 11:2**

> Know ye not that your bodies are the members of Christ? shall I then take the members of Christ, and make *them* the members of an harlot? God forbid.
> **1 Corinthians 6:15**

There are other names used to describe the church and, while I am concentrating on Ephesians and 1 Corinthians written by Paul, a moving description of the church compared to a widow is presented in a paper written by Horatius Bonar in 1867 titled "The Church's Widowhood" based on Luke 18:3.

To summarize, a church is not a building or physical locality. If a believer does not come to the physical building or church services, he or she is still part of the church. If a church building were to be destroyed, that church still exists. Church is clearly a shared belief and behavior amongst individuals who pattern their lives after the teachings and works of Jesus Christ.

To follow Christ is to be part of the body of Christ, the congregation, made up of men and women, regardless of race, is likened to the wife of Christ and Christ as her husband. We best protect the congregation by individually following the teachings and actions of Christ.

Chapter 4

"The head of the woman *is* the man"

The inspiration that became this book was to study the words of Paul in Ephesians and 1 Corinthians and to discover their true meaning. In the previous chapters, we have examined what church is and have looked at the use of allegory, parable, and similitude in the Bible. Now Let's look at Paul's meaning and use of the word "woman." After the following Bible verses, there will be commentary to clarify the meaning. You may find it helpful to follow along with your KJV Standard Bible while you read (that Bible can also be found online at https://www.kingjamesbibleonline.org/). The verses that follow are the ones that require greater clarification.

But I would have you know, that the head of every man is Christ;

and the head of the woman *is* the man; and the head of Christ *is* God.

1 Corinthians 11:3

First Corinthians 11:3 tells us where mankind fits into God's power structure. God is the head of Christ. Christ is the head of the spiritual infinite church. Man is the head of the physical church, and we are to love and protect the church by each individual believer following the teachings of Christ.

God

Christ

Man

Church

Paul is telling us that an institution called a "church" is not above us. Only Christ and God the Father are above us. The church, or woman, is the body and bride of Christ. While individual and local gatherings of believers can be called a "church," we are all individually meant to be under the teachings of Christ, and no institution should replace that. God the Creator, Christ the begotten of God, mankind as created by God, and the church or fellowship of man under the teachings of Christ, also known as the body of Christ. Christ is the head of the spiritual body, but man is the head of the physical church.

For the husband is the head of the wife, even as Christ is the head
of the church: and he is the saviour of the body."
Ephesians 5:23

But to us *there is* but one God, the Father, of whom *are* all things, and we in him; and one Lord Jesus Christ, by whom *are* all things, and we by him.
1 Corinthians 8:6

The following are the verses in 1 Corinthians 8:6 above put in an easier to read format.
One God the Father
Of whom *are* all things
We *in* Him
One Lord Jesus Christ
By whom *are* all things
We *by* Him

For as the woman *is* of the man, even so *is* the man also by the woman;
but all things of God.
1 Corinthians 11:12

The above verse is telling us:
The body of Christ, the church, is composed of individual followers of Christ

By the teachings of Christ
All in God.

Let's take a journey through Ephesians. Paul is writing to the saints of Ephesus about the "mystery of Christ," which is to bring salvation to all people through faith in Christ and bring them into the body of Christ. Interpretation will follow the verses.

And to make all *men* see what *is* the fellowship of the mystery, which from the beginning of the world hath been hid in God, who created all things by Jesus Christ.
Ephesians 3:9

Now therefore ye are no more strangers and foreigners, but fellow citizens with the saints, and of the household of God;

And are built upon the foundation of the apostles and prophets, Jesus Christ himself being the chief corner *stone*;

In whom all the building fitly framed together groweth unto an holy temple in the Lord:

In whom ye also are builded together for an habitation of God through the Spirit.
Ephesians 2:19-22

Paul is saying in the verses above that the body of Christ is the temple of the Lord.

That in the dispensation of the fulness of times he might gather together in one all things in Christ, both which are in heaven, and which are on earth; *even* in him.
Ephesians 1:10

Paul is talking about the mystery of Christ and the church.

Now we are going to look at Ephesians 5:19-33. Keep in mind a key verse that defines what Paul is telling us: *"This is a great mystery: but I speak concerning Christ and the church."* Ephesians 5:32

19 Speaking to yourselves in psalms and hymns and spiritual songs, singing and
making melody in your heart to the Lord;
20 Giving thanks always for all things unto God and the Father in the name
of our Lord Jesus Christ;
21 Submitting yourselves one to another in the fear of God.
22 Wives, submit yourselves unto your own husbands, as unto the Lord.

23 For the husband is the head of the wife, even as Christ is the head of the church: and he is the saviour of the body.
Ephesians 5:19-23

The above verses tell us that man is the head of the earthly church and while humans were not created for the church, they are one body and part of each other. This is important as it supports freedom and the God-given rights of mankind. But we are to love the body of Christ as ourselves. Let's continue with Ephesians 5: 27-33.

27 That he might present it to himself a glorious church, not having spot, or wrinkle, or any such thing; but that it should be holy and without blemish.
28 So ought men to love their wives as their own bodies. He that loveth his wife loveth himself.
29 For no man ever yet hated his own flesh; but nourisheth and cherisheth it, even as the Lord the church:
30 For we are members of his body, of his flesh, and of his bones.

31 For this cause shall a man leave his father and mother, and shall be joined unto his wife, and they shall be one flesh.

32 This is a great mystery: but I speak concerning Christ and the Church.

33 Nevertheless let every one of you in particular so love his wife even as himself; and the wife *see* that she reverence *her* husband.

Ephesians 5:27-33

Paul uses woman and wife as a similitude, meaning resemblance, for church and uses husband as a similitude for Christ and His teachings. We are to leave our mother and father and join the church or body of Christ. So why does Paul use woman and wife as a similitude for the church or body of Christ? Paul is protecting the teachings of Jesus and protecting his ministry. Remember the times that Paul lived in; that his ministry and his life were threatened by the religious leaders and current government he lived under. Can you think of any churches that have become more like an institution than the body of Christ following the teachings and actions of Jesus? Paul uses this same language in 1 Corinthians, which we will look at in the next chapter.

Chapter 5

Hair and Covering: "For a man indeed ought not to cover *his* head"

In 1 Corinthians Paul is writing to the believers in Corinth because of the divisions among them, referring to them as still babes in Christ and carnal. Paul says the church should follow his teachings because he is following Jesus. We are going to be looking at verses from 1 Corinthians and Ephesians, with commentary after the verses to clarify Paul's words.

Be ye followers of me, even as I also *am* of Christ.
1 Corinthians 11:1

Now I beseech you, brethren, by the name of our Lord Jesus Christ, that ye all speak the same thing, and *that* there be no divisions among you; but *that* ye be perfectly joined together in the same mind and in the same judgment.
1 Corinthians 1:10

In the above passages, Paul gives all the glory to Jesus and encourages the brethren to follow his example because he follows Christ. Paul says this to address the divisions amongst them.

> It is reported commonly *that* there is fornication among you, and such fornication as is not so much as named among the Gentiles, that you should have his father's wife.
> **1 Corinthians 5:1**

In the above verse, Paul is using fornication as a similitude for worshipping false gods. Idolatry is the worship of an object as though it were a deity, but worse is to be a fornicator and lust after and take part in false doctrine, causing you to worship in fellowship as part of a false church. You cannot worship Christ and God while also worshipping another God with different teachings. This spiritual sin is worse than other carnal sins. In Paul's time , the Roman Empire was polytheistic and worshipped multiple gods and goddesses.

What? Know ye not that he which is joined to an harlot is one body? for two, saith he, shall be one flesh.
1 Corinthians 6:16

Harlot is used above to represent a false church following false teachings. Note how Paul uses the phrase "one flesh" and how the following verse, Ephesians 5:31, helps us define the meaning.

For this cause shall a man leave his father and mother, and shall be joined unto his wife, and they two shall be one flesh.

This is a great mystery: but I speak concerning Christ and the church.
Ephesians 5:31, 32

In the verse above, Paul is using wife as a similitude for church, the body of Christ. Now let's journey back to 1 Corinthians 5:2 and listen to what more Paul has to say about false teachings.

And ye are puffed up, and have not rather mourned, that he that hath done this deed might be taken away and from among you.

For I verily, as absent in body, but present in spirit, have judged already, as though I were present, *concerning* him that hath so done this deed,

In the name of our Lord Jesus Christ, when ye are gathered together, and my spirit, with the power of our Lord Jesus Christ,

To deliver such an one unto Satan for the destruction of the flesh, that the spirit may be saved in the day of the Lord Jesus.

Your glorying *is* not good. Know ye not that a little leaven leaveneth the whole lump?
1 Corinthians 5:2-6

Paul is saying above that glorifying any other than Christ and his teachings is defiling the teachings of Jesus and bringing false teachings, referred to as leaven, into the body of Christ. Paul talks more about leaven in the following verses.

Purge out therefore the old leaven, that ye may be a new lump, as ye are unleavened. For even Christ our Passover is sacrificed for us:

Therefore let us keep the feast, not with old leaven, neither with the leaven of malice and wickedness; but with the unleavened *bread* of sincerity and truth.

I wrote unto you in an epistle not to company with fornicators:

Yet not altogether with the fornicators of this world, or with the covetous, or extortioners, or with idolaters; for then must ye needs go out of the world.

But now I have written unto you not to keep company, if any man that is called a brother be a fornicator, or covetous, or an idolater, or a railer, or a drunkard, or an extortioner; with such an one no not to eat.

For what have I to do to judge them also that are without? do not ye judge them that are within?

But them that are without God judgeth. Therefore put away from among yourselves that wicked person.
1 Corinthians 5:7-13

In the above verses, Paul is talking about keeping leaven, which represents false teachings, out of the church. Paul also refers to leaven as old teachings and is saying that we are to follow Jesus Christ who came preaching and living a New Testament and died for us. While Paul says you must go among the sinners in the world to preach, you are not to bring false teachings into the church. The real teachings of sincerity and truth should not be corrupted with false teachings of malice and wickedness. While we are to judge our actions within the body of the church, it is up to God to judge those outside the church.

> Meats for the belly, and the belly for meats: but God shall destroy both it and them. Now the body *is* not for fornication, but for the Lord; and the Lord for the body.
> **1 Corinthians 6:13**

In this verse, Paul is saying that the body of Christ, the church, is for the Lord and the Lord is for the body of Christ. The body of Christ should not follow false teachings.

> And God hath both raised up the Lord, and will also raise up us by his own power,

> Know ye not that your bodies are the members of Christ? Shall I then take the members of Christ, and make *them* the members of an harlot? God forbid.
> **1 Corinthians 6:14-15**

In the above verse, harlot refers to an apostate or false church with false teachings.

> What? Know ye not that he which is joined to an harlot is one body? for two, saith he, shall be one flesh.
>
> But he that is joined unto the Lord is one spirit.
>
> Flee fornication. Every sin that a man doeth is without the body; but he that committeth fornication sinneth against his own body.
> **1 Corinthians 6:16-18**

The verses above say that what we worship becomes part of us and we become part of that fellowship. Notice the use of the term "one flesh." The individual sins a person commits are individual, but bringing false teachings into the church is a sin against the church, the body of Christ.

What? Know ye not that your body is the temple of the Holy Ghost *which is* in you, which ye have of God, and ye are not your own?

For ye are bought with a price: therefore glorify God in your body, and in your spirit, which are God's.
1 Corinthians 6:19-20

Paul is speaking of the "mystery of Christ" and as believers and followers of Christ, we are the body of Christ, which we refer to as church and congregation. Individually, and as the body of Christ, we are the temple of the Holy Ghost. In Chapter 4 of this book, we learned in Ephesians 2:19-22 that the body of Christ, from all over the world, is the holy temple of the Lord. Believers are to glorify God in the body of Christ, which joined together is one spirit.

In 1 Corinthians chapter 11, Paul writes to the Corinthians similarly as he does to the Ephesians as discussed in chapter 4. However, in Paul's letter to Corinth, he also talks about hair and covering and admonishes them about their various practices in the church. Remember that one reason Paul is writing to the Corinthians is because of the disagreements among them.

Be ye followers of me, even as I also *am* of Christ.

Now I praise you, brethren, that ye remember me in all things, and keep the ordinances, as I delivered *them* to you.

But I would have you know, that the head of every man is Christ; and the head of the woman *is* the man; and the head of Christ *is* God.
1 Corinthians 11:1-3

This is a great mystery: but I speak concerning Christ and the church.
Ephesians 5:32

Paul tells us where mankind fits into God's power structure:
God
Christ
Man
Church
Paul is telling us that an institution called a "church" is not above us. Only Christ and God are above us. The church, or woman, is the body and wife of Christ. While individual and local gather-ings of believers can be called a local church, we are all individually meant to be under the teachings of Christ and no institution should replace that. God

the Creator, Christ the begotten of God, mankind as created by God and then the church, which is the fellowship of man under the teachings of Christ also known as the body of Christ, comprised of believers worldwide.

Let's define a few concepts before we go through the very confusing issue of hair and covering. First, let's remember that Paul is addressing disagreements in the church. When Paul wrote to the saints of Ephesus, he did not address head coverings because there was no disagreement among them. Paul's letter to the Corinthians emphasizes disagreements among them. In that time there was a Jewish custom for men to cover their heads as a sign of humility before God, and women covered their heads as evidence of modesty before men. Married women would cover their hair or have it shorn. Single women would have long hair uncovered as a symbol of innocence and purity. These are customs of men and not of God. Paul goes on to say that there is no such custom in following Christ. Christians generally prayed bareheaded. Let's remember the miracle of the loaves and fishes when Jesus fed the multitude and remember the interpretation Jesus gave to his disciples.

How is it that ye do not understand that I spake *it* not to you concerning bread, that ye should be aware of the leaven of the Pharisees and of the Sadducees?
Matthew 16:11

The covering of the head is still a contested issue among reform and orthodox Jewry. The physical act of covering the hair was not important according to Paul, and Paul goes on to give a spiritual meaning of hair, head, and covering, but we need to explore a few topics before we can understand those verses.

Long Hair

Long hair stands for purity; to walk with God and to follow His teachings. Long hair is a glory covering and commitment to the teaching and works of Christ. Head covering is an expression of submission and obedience to the headship of Christ in the church. Long hair was the head covering given to the church by angels, to consecrate it and protect it. These concepts will be explained more fully through the following verses.

Nazarite Vow

For, lo, thou shalt conceive, and bear a son; and no razor shall come upon his head: for the child shall be a Nazarite unto God from the womb: and he shall begin to deliver Israel out of the hand of the Philistines.
Judges 13:5

And the woman bare a son, and called his name Samson: and the child grew, and the LORD blessed him.
Judges 13:24

That he told her all his heart, and said unto her, There hath not come a razor upon mine head; for I *have been* a Nazarite unto God from my mother's womb: if I be shaven, then my strength will go from me, and I shall become weak, and be like any *other* man.
Judges 16:17

And the LORD spake unto Moses, saying,

Speak unto the children of Israel, and say unto them, When either man or woman shall separate *themselves* to vow of a Nazarite, to separate *themselves* unto the LORD:

He shall separate *himself* from wine and strong drink, and shall drink no vinegar of wine, or vinegar of strong drink, neither shall he drink any liquor of grapes, nor eat moist grapes, or dried.

All the days of his separation shall he eat nothing that is made of the vine tree, from the kernels even to the husk.

All the days of the vow of his separation there shall no razor come upon his head: until the days be fulfilled, in the which he separateth *himself* unto the LORD, he shall be holy, *and* shall let the locks of the hair of his head grow.
Numbers 6:1-5

And this is the law of the Nazarite, when the days of his separation are fulfilled: he shall be brought unto the door of the tabernacle of the congregation.
Numbers 6:13

And the Nazarite shall shave the head of his separation *at* the door of the tabernacle of the congregation, and shall take the hair of the head of his separation, and put *it* in the fire which *is* under the sacrifice of the peace offerings.

And the priest shall take the sodden shoulder of the ram, and one unleavened cake out of the basket, and one unleavened wafer, and shall put *them* upon the hands of the Nazarite, after *the hair* of his separation is shaven:

And the priest shall wave them *for* a wave offering before the LORD; this *is* holy for the priest, with the wave breast and heave shoulder; and after that the Nazarite may drink wine.

This *is* the law of the Nazarite who hath vowed, *and* of his offering unto the LORD for his separation, beside *that* that his hand shall get: according to the vow which he vowed, so he must do after the law of his separation.
Numbers 6:18-21

Consecration

The origin for the word *consecration* comes from the Latin root consecrate, which means dedication, devoted, and sacred. Consecration means an association with the sacred. Sacred means to be set apart for worship or service. Once something is consecrated, it is made holy and is then able to be used for religious ceremonies.

In the case of hair and a vow, you cleanse yourself before coming before the Lord to pray and ask forgiveness. Short hair or shaving the hair was an act of cleansing yourself. After taking the vow, Nazarites let their hair grow long to show their separation to the Lord, which was a symbol of purity and adherence to their vow. After the fulfillment of days of the vow, the consecrated hair was shaved or removed for secular or worldly use in a religious ceremony. In the case of the Nazarite vow, the hair was burned for a peace offering.

> And Paul *after this* tarried *there* yet a good while, and then took his leave of the brethren, and sailed thence into Syria, and with him Priscilla and Aquila; having shorn *his* head in Cenchrea: for he had a vow. **Acts 18:18**

Paul shaving his head in Acts 18:18 doesn't mean he took a Nazarite vow or was a Nazarite, but the concept of Paul shaving his head as a commitment to the Lord seems reasonable and shows he was very familiar with spiritual meanings of hair.

Other Meanings of Cover

Covering is also a form of protection as used by

Jesus in the form of parables and allegory. To cut or shave the hair or to be shorn was also used as a symbol of cleansing, to be uncovered and repent and washed free of sin.

Putting It All Together

In Ephesians Paul writes to the Saints of Ephesus, and while he talks about the hierarchy; God, Christ, Man and Church, he does not discuss the head covering. This appears to be because of the division amongst those in Corinth about the practice of physically covering the hair. Paul says it does not matter and goes on to explain the spiritual significance.

Church is the body of Christ, a congregation of believers from around the world that follow the teachings and acts of Christ. The blood and body of Christ are his New Testament teaching and works. The body of Christ is also referred to as a woman, bride, and wife. A false church is often referred to as a harlot and whore.

The adherence to Christ of the individual brings about the strength of the community which brings about the strength of the body.

God is the head of Christ, Christ is the head of

man and the spiritual body, while man (mankind) is the head of the earthly church.

An individual may sin, requiring the need to cleanse by coming before God to pray and ask forgiveness.

The Word of God is never in need of humility or forgiveness. Jesus and His teachings are perfect and never in need of being cleansed (shorn) or considered unclean or needing forgiveness. The Word of God is true now and forever.

The (church, body, woman) in its purest form is complete understanding, faith and fellowship with Christ without sin. It is the message of Christ, the Law, teachings and acts of Christ and not of man. We are sinners and not perfect.

> Every man praying or prophesying, having *his* head covered, dishonoureth his head.
> **1 Corinthians 11:4**

The head of man (mankind) is Christ. Be faithful and truthful to Christ with reverence and humility. Paul is speaking carnally, humans should not be ashamed by the headship of Christ and not ashamed they are human, as they are created In God and by Christ. Physically men and women do not need to cover their heads. Spiritually we are to confess and be naked before God, confessing and not hiding our sins.

> But every woman that prayeth or prophesieth with *her* head uncovered dishonoureth her head: for that is even all one as if she were shaven.
> **1 Corinthians 11:5**

In the above verse, Paul is speaking spiritually. Long hair is the head covering given by angels. The covering of the church are the teachings and works of Christ and her glory covering. Long hair symbolizes the purity of the teachings and headship of Christ. The church, or body of Christ, should be modest and follow the teachings of Christ.

> For if the woman be not covered, let her also be shorn: but if it be a shame for a woman to be shorn or shaven, let her be covered.
> **1 Corinthians 11:6**

If the church's teachings are not consistent with the teachings of Christ, then let her false teachings be uncovered and cleansed. Her hair is her glory and covering. A physical woman need not be shorn or shaven for her hair is also her glory given to her by God.

> For a man indeed ought not to cover *his* head, forasmuch as he is the image and glory of God: but the woman is the glory of the man.
> **1 Corinthians 11:7**

For a human indeed ought not to cover his head because he is the glory of God, but the church is the glory of the man. Christ is the head of man and the spiritual church; man is the head of the physical church. The congregation, the body of Christ, should show humility before God but the perfect teachings of Christ are covered by the glory covering.

> For the man is not of the woman; but the woman of the man.

> Neither was the man created for the woman; but the woman for the man.

> For this cause ought the woman to have power on *her* head because of the angels.

> Nevertheless neither is the man without the woman, neither the woman without the man, in the Lord.

For as the woman *is* of the man, even so *is* the man
also by the woman; but all things of God.
1 Corinthians 11:8-12

As in Ephesians, Paul is saying that man is over
the earthly church, that man was not created for the
church, but they were created for each other. This is
somewhat like man was not created for the sabbath
but sabbath was created for man. The church is
made up of individual believers, but the individual
believers also become the union of the body. The
adherence to the teachings of Christ by the individual brings about the strength of the family, which
brings about the strength of the community, which
brings about the strength of the body of Christ. Man
is stronger together than apart and everyone that
follows Christ is one spiritual body.

Judge in yourselves: is it comely that a woman pray
unto God uncovered?
1 Corinthians 11:13

Paul is saying that hair is her covering given to
her by the angels.

Doth not even nature itself teach you, that, if a man have long hair, it is a shame unto him?

But if a woman have long hair, it is a glory to her: for *her* hair is given her for a covering.

But if any man seem to be contentious, we have no such custom, neither the churches of God.
1 Corinthians 11:14-16

To physically cover your head or not should not be a disagreement in the church. This is along the lines that circumcision or uncircumcision does not matter physically but it is the circumcision of the heart that matters to God. A physical woman does not need to cut her hair or cover her head. The body of Christ should be modest and show humility and reverence to God and Christ. Paul talks about the carnal and spiritual aspects of hair covering at the same time, which was difficult for the church in Corinth to understand and even more confusing for us to understand 2,000 years later. Paul says there should be no division in the church over physically covering your hair. Covering the physical head is a custom of man and not a teaching of Christ.

Why doesn't Paul just come straight out and say what he means? Paul says in Corinthians and Ephesians that he knows this is hard to understand and a great mystery, but he is speaking concerning Christ and the church. We know that earthly matters are often used to convey spiritual matters, and we need to consider the time Paul lived in: Christ was crucified, and Christianity was not yet accepted but persecuted. The protective covering of Paul's teaching was to convey the meaning without inciting the wrath of the Sadducees and Pharisees and powers of Rome, causing the termination of his ministry. Just as Jesus spoke in parables to protect His teachings and hide them from those who did not believe and follow the Word of God but would rather destroy it. Continuing in 1 Corinthians, Paul has more to say to the church in Corinth.

> Now in this that I declare *unto you* I praise *you* not, that ye come together not for the better, but for the worse.

> For first of all, when ye come together in the church, I hear that there be divisions among you; and I partly believe it.

> For there must be also heresies among you, that they which are approved may be made manifest among you.

When ye come together therefore into one place, *this* is not to eat the Lord's supper.

For in eating every one taketh before *other* his own supper: and one is hungry, and another is drunken.

What? Have ye not houses to eat and to drink in? or despise ye the church of God, and shame them that have not? What shall I say to you? Shall I praise you in this? I praise *you* not.

For I have received of the Lord that which also I delivered unto you, that the Lord Jesus the *same* night in which he was betrayed took bread:

And when he had given thanks, he brake *it*, and said, Take, eat: this is my body, which is broken for you: this do in remembrance of me.

After the same manner also *he took* the cup, when he had supped, saying, This cup is the new testament in my blood: this do ye, as oft as ye drink *it*, in remembrance of me.

For as often as ye eat this bread, and drink this cup, ye do shew the Lord's death till he come.

Wherefore whosoever shall eat this bread, and drink *this* cup of the Lord, unworthily, shall be guilty of the body and blood of the Lord.

But let a man examine himself, and so let him eat of *that* bread, and drink of *that* cup.

For he that eateth and drinketh unworthily, eateth and drinketh damnation to himself, not discerning the Lord's body.

For this cause many *are* weak and sickly among you, and many sleep.

For if we would judge ourselves, we should not be judged.

But when we are judged, we are chastened of the Lord, that we should not be condemned with the world.

Wherefore, my brethren, when ye come together to eat, tarry one for another.

And if any man hunger, let him eat at home; that ye come not together unto condemnation. And the rest will I set in order when I come.
1 Corinthians 11:17-34

Paul is discussing the sanctity of the Lord's supper and our remembrance of it. The blood and body of Christ are spiritually symbolic of his New Testament teachings and his sacrifice for us on the cross. When we come together to remember the Lords's supper, we show the Lord's death until he returns. Jesus did break physical bread and sup with his disciples, but when we come together in re-membrance, we are coming together to share spir-itual food, and the physical food is to be eaten with moderation and with charity. We are to share this remembrance in reverence until the second coming of our Lord.

Chapter 6

"Let your women keep silence in the churches."

In 1 Corinthians chapters 12 through 15, Paul talks more about the body of Christ and says that every individual that makes up the church is given different gifts and while the gifts are all different, they are all equally important in making up the whole body of Christ. Paul uses the similitude of our own body parts as a tool to explain the body of Christ. Let's start our journey with 1 Corinthians 12:1-13.

> Now concerning spiritual *gifts*, brethren, I would not have you ignorant.
>
> Ye know that ye were Gentiles, carried away unto these dumb idols, even as ye were led.
>
> Wherefore I give you to understand, that no man speaking by the Spirit of God calleth Jesus accursed: and *that* no man can say that Jesus is the Lord, but by the Holy Ghost.

Now there are diversities of gifts, but the same Spirit.

And there are differences of administrations, but the same Lord.

And there are diversities of operations, but it is the same God which worketh all in all.

But the manifestation of the Spirit is given to every man to profit withal.

For to one is given by the Spirit the word of wisdom; to another the word of knowledge by the same Spirit;

To another faith by the same Spirit; to another the gifts of healing of the same Spirit;

To another the working of miracles; to another prophecy; to another discerning of spirits; to another *divers* kinds of tongues; to another the interpretation of tongues:

But all these worketh that one and the selfsame Spirit, dividing to every man severally as he will.

For as the body is one, and hath many members, and all the members of that one body, being many, are one body: so also *is* Christ.

For by one Spirit are we all baptized into one body, whether *we* be Jews or Gentiles, whether *we* be bond

WOMAN AS CREATED BY GOD

or free; and have been all made to drink into one spirit.

1 Corinthians 12:1-13

Paul is saying in the above verses that men, women, all of humanity are one spirit, who believe in Jesus Christ, and in this shared belief are one body. Let's continue with 1 Corinthians 12:14 as Paul explains this further.

For the body is not one member, but many.

If the foot shall say, Because I am not the hand, I am not of the body; is it therefore not of the body?

And if the ear shall say, Because I am not the eye, I am not of the body; is it therefore not of the body?

If the whole body *were* an eye, where *were* the hearing? If the whole *were* hearing, where *were* the smelling?

But now hath God set the members every one of them in the body, as it hath pleased him.

And if they were all one member, where *were* the body?

But now *are they* many members, yet but one body.

- 47 -

And the eye cannot say unto the hand, I have no need of thee: nor again the head to the feet, I have no need of you.

Nay, much more those members of the body, which seem to be more feeble, are necessary:

And those *members* of the body, which we think to be less honourable, upon these we bestow more abundant honour; and our uncomely *parts* have more abundant comeliness,

For our comely *parts* have no need: but God hath tempered the body together, having given more abundant honour to that *part* which lacked:

That there should be no schism in the body; but *that* the members should have the same care one for another.

And whether one member suffer, all the members suffer with it; or one member be honoured, all the members rejoice with it.

Now ye are the body of Christ, and members in particular.

And God hath set some in the church, first apostles, secondarily prophets, thirdly teachers, after that miracles, then gifts of healings, helps, governments, diversities of tongues.

Are all apostles? *are* all prophets? *are* all teachers? *are* all workers of miracles?

Have all the gifts of healing? Do all speak with tongues? Do all interpret?

But covet earnestly the best gifts: and yet shew I unto you a more excellent way.
1 Corinthians 12:14-31

In the above verses, Paul is saying that all the gifts given to us by God are equally important, but we esteem some gifts to be more important than others. Paul explains that all these different gifts are necessary for the body of Christ just like all your individual body parts are necessary for your human body to function. Paul says there is something greater to strive for in 1 Corinthians 13. The most important qualities a human can strive to have, regardless of gifts, is hope, faith, and charity and the greatest of these is charity.

Charity suffereth long, *and* is kind; charity envieth not; charity vaunteth not itself, is not puffed up,

Doth not behave itself unseemly, seeketh not her own, is not easily provoked, thinketh no evil;

Rejoiceth not in iniquity, but rejoiceth in the truth;

Beareth all things, believeth all things, hopeth all things, endureth all things.

Charity never faileth: but whether *there be* prophecies, they shall fail; whether *there be* tongues, they shall cease; whether *there be* knowledge, it shall vanish away.

For we know in part, and we prophesy in part.

But when that which is perfect is come, then that which is in part shall be done away.

When I was a child, I spake as a child, I understood as a child, I thought as a child: but when I became a man, I put away childish things.

For now we see through a glass, darkly; but then face to face: now I know in part; but then shall I know even as also I am known.

And now abideth faith, hope, charity, these three; but the greatest of these *is* charity.

1 Corinthians 13:4-13

In 1 Corinthians chapter 14, Paul goes on to instruct us on how we should behave when we come together to worship. From what Paus says, speaking in tongues was an esteemed gift. However, Paul says that a lot of people talking in tongues without an interpreter sounds like a bunch of gibberish and does nothing to edify the body. Rather, pray for the gift of prophecy because prophecy edifies the body.

But if all prophesy, and there come in one that believeth not, or *one* unlearned, he is convinced of all, he is judged of all:

And thus are the secrets of his heart made manifest; and so falling down on *his* face he will worship God, and report that God is in you of a truth.

1 Corinthians 14:24-25

Paul goes on to tell us how to behave when we come together to worship.

How is it then, brethren? When ye come together, every one of you hath a psalm, hath a doctrine, hath a tongue, hath a revelation, hath an interpretation. Let all things be done unto edifying.

If any man speak in an *unknown* tongue, *let it be* by two, or at the most *by* three, and *that* by course; and let one interpret.

But if there be no interpreter, let him keep silence in the church; and let him speak to himself, and to God.

Let the prophets speak two or three, and let the other judge.

If *anything* be revealed to another that sitteth by, let the first hold his peace.

For ye may all prophesy one by one, that all may learn, and all may be comforted.

And the spirits of the prophets are subject to the prophets.

For God is not *the author* of confusion, but of peace, as in all churches of the saints.
1 Corinthians 14:26-33

In most churches today, the congregation sits quietly and listens to the preacher. And this is what

Paul is talking about. The body of the church, the woman, all speaking at once, whether in tongues or prophesying or shouting out of doctrine is chaotic and not given to edification. Instead, the body of Christ, men and women, should remain quiet in church or take turns speaking in an orderly fashion. It appears that in Paul's time church was a little more participatory.

> Let your women keep silence in the churches: for it is not permitted unto them to speak; but *they are commanded* to be under obedience, as also saith the law.
>
> And if they will learn anything, let them ask their husbands at home: for it is a shame for women to speak in the church.
>
> What? Came the word of God out from you? Or came it unto you only?
> **1 Corinthians 14:34-36**

Women and husbands, as used above, refer to the local church and how to conduct ourselves in church. The woman is the body of Christ, and the husband is the Word of God, which you are to study at home or with your learned pastor, preacher, or teacher. Again, this is how we conduct ourselves in church today and, as Paul says, God is not the author of confusion. This interpretation is consistent with the entire message that Paul is giving and is important when large groups gather to worship. "But if there be no interpreter, let him keep silence in the church; and let him speak to himself, and to God" 1 Corinthians 14:28.

Just like Paul used human body parts to explain the body of Christ, Paul is using similitudes of the family to explain how we should conduct ourselves in church.

> If any man think himself to be a prophet, or spiritual, let him acknowledge that the things that I write unto you are the commandments of the Lord.
>
> But if any man be ignorant, let him be ignorant.
>
> Wherefore, brethren, covet to prophesy, and forbid not to speak with tongues.
>
> Let all things be done decently and in order.
> **1 Corinthians 14:37-40**

To summarize, coming together to worship should not be chaotic but orderly and for the edification of all. If you have a prophesy or understanding or speak in tongues, present it in an orderly way before the congregation.

In 1 Corinthians 15, Paul addresses Christ risen.

And when all things shall be subdued unto him, then shall the Son also himself be subject unto him that put all things under him, that God may be all in all.
1 Corinthians:15:28

In a moment, in the twinkling of an eye, at the last trump: for the trumpet shall sound,

and the dead shall be raised incorruptible, and we shall be changed.

For this corruptible must put on incorruption, and this mortal *must* put on immortality.

So when this corruptible shall have put on incorruption, and this mortal shall have put on immortality, then shall be brought to pass the saying that is written, Death is swallowed up in victory.

O death, where *is* thy sting? O grave, where *is* thy victory?

The sting of death *is* sin; and the strength of sin *is* the law.

But thanks be to God, which giveth us the victory through our Lord Jesus Christ.

Therefore, my beloved brethren, be ye steadfast, unmoveable, always abounding in the work of the Lord, forasmuch as ye know that your labour is not in vain in the Lord.
1 Corinthians 15:52-58

In the above verses Paul proves our faith. Christ did rise from the dead. If Christ is not risen our faith is in vain. There is an earthly body and there is a spiritual body. God has given Christ power over everything. Christ will subdue all enemies and the last enemy to be subdued will be death. The cause of death is sin because God is truth and law, but sin has been conquered through our Lord Jesus Christ on the cross. When Christ subdues all the enemies our earthly, corruptible, and mortal body will become our heavenly, incorruptible, and immortal body and then even Christ shall be subject unto God, that God may be all in all.

Chapter 7

Between a Man and a Woman

As we have explored in chapters 4, 5, and 6 of this book, Paul has been talking about the church. In 1 Corinthians chapter 7, Paul discusses the relationship between a physical man and a physical woman. First Corinthians chapter 7 is self-explanatory and a short chapter so I would suggest reading it all the way through in your Bible. I am going to give a short synopsis with some supporting verses at the end of this chapter.

There isn't any conclusive research to support whether Paul was ever married. Theologians have varying opinions, some saying he never was married and others saying that a learned Pharisee of his time would have been expected to be married and that Paul may have released his wife after his conversion. I can only go by what Paul says of himself at the time he wrote to Corinth and at that time he had committed himself to God and was His servant and not married.

Paul says not everyone is called to be celibate as

he had been called. If a man or woman wishes to be intimate and have sex, he or she should have a husband or wife. As far as how they should treat each other, Paul says: "Let the husband render unto the wife due benevolence; and likewise also the wife unto the husband." 1 Corinthians 7:3

Paul goes on to say that if either a man or a woman is a widow or a virgin, it is fine if you choose not to marry and makes it easier for you to serve the Lord. If you choose to marry, there will be times of trouble. Time is short and the troubles we have in this world will pass. Every man and woman have their own talents and are all called to serve God in various ways.

Now concerning the things whereof ye wrote unto me: *It is* good for a man not to touch a woman.

Nevertheless, to *avoid* fornication, let every man have his own wife, and let every woman have her own husband.

Let the husband render unto the wife due benevolence: and likewise also the wife unto the husband.

The wife hath not power of her own body, but the husband: and likewise also the husband hath not power of his own body, but the wife.

Brethren, let every man, wherein he is called, therein abide with God.
1 Corinthians 7:1-4, 24

Chapter 8

The Fellowship of the Mystery

And to make all *men* see what *is* the fellowship of the mystery, which from the beginning of the world hath been hid in God, who created all things by Jesus Christ.
Ephesians 3:9

Imagine yourself walking down the streets of Corinth in the time of Paul the Apostle. The gentiles were not accepted by the Jews who considered themselves the chosen people of God through the Old Testament. Jesus had come to fulfill the Old Testament, die for our sins, and give us a New Testament. We can pick up the New Testament and read it for understanding, but the New Testament did not exist as a book at the time.

Paul and the apostles were spreading the gospel of Jesus, and their actions, teachings, and testimony of Jesus form our New Testament. The idea that believing gentiles were now part of the chosen of God and the body of Christ, as branches grafted onto the tree, was something they were just grappling to understand. Paul's letters to Corinth and Ephesus deal with the mystery of "Christ and the church" and the "fellowship of the mystery." "This is a great mystery: but I speak concerning Christ and the church." Ephesians 5:32

Paul used similitudes like women and hair to disguise his teachings and to protect his ministry from hostile authorities as we explored in chapters 4, 5 and 6 of this book. The "fellowship of the mystery" and the mystery of "Christ and the church" are about the body of Christ, also known as the church, wife, bride and woman. Let's explore the deeper meaning of the mystery.

> And call no *man* your father upon the earth: for one is your Father, which is in heaven.
> **Matthew 23:9**

> So God created man in his *own* image, in the image of God created he him; male and female created he them.
> **Genesis 1:27**

> But from the beginning of the creation God made them male and female.
> **Mark 10:6**

Declaring the end from the beginning, and from ancient times *the things* that are not *yet* done, saying, My counsel shall stand, and I will do all my pleasure.
Isaiah 46:10

That in the dispensation of the fulness of times he might gather together in one all things in Christ, both which are in heaven, and which are on earth; *even* in him.
Ephesians 1:10

And when all things shall be subdued unto him, then shall the Son also himself be subject unto him that put all things under him, that God may be all in all.
Corinthians 15:28

These verses above tell us that God is our Father and God wanted us with Him, so He created man and woman in His image. God knew the end from the beginning and knew that man would sin but wanted us through love, understanding, and respect like a physical man and wife are joined together through love, understanding and respect, which means God gave us free choice to follow Him or not.

The New Testament gives every man and woman, and every human on earth created by God entry into His heavenly kingdom through faith in

Jesus Christ and His teachings. Jesus and His teachings are the way to the Father, and you are His holy temple through faith. Before the crucifixion and resurrection of Christ, the idea that all people could be the chosen people of God would have been unheard of.

> And if some of the branches be broken off, and thou, being a wild olive tree, wert graffed in among them, and with them partakest of the root and fatness of the olive tree.
> **Romans 11:17**

> Let both grow together until the harvest: and in the time of harvest I will say to the reapers, Gather ye together first the tares, and bind them in bundles to burn them: but gather the wheat into my barn.
> **Matthew 13:30**

God is patient in his suffering until the fullness of time when all those in Christ are accounted for. Our suffering in this world will be but a distant fleeting memory when compared to our immortal life with Christ in God. What God has prepared for us is beyond our imagination.

For as the body is one, and hath many members, and all the members of the body, being many, are one body: so also *is* Christ.
1 Corinthians 12:12

Who will you follow? Will you follow the father of lies or the Father of truth? First, we choose whom we will follow, then believers together become the body of Christ. We grow the body of Christ first by growing ourselves in Christ through our thoughts and actions towards ourselves, other people, and our influence in the world. We grow the body of Christ by coming together as a physical man and woman to create new life to nurture in the fellowship of God. We grow the body of Christ and make it stronger by coming together as believers following Christ. We grow the body of Christ by loving our enemies and living the teachings of Christ.

For we are labourers together with God: ye are God's husbandry, *ye are* God's building.
1 Corinthians 3:9

If any man defile the temple of God, him shall God destroy; for the temple of God is holy, which *temple* ye are.
1 Corinthians 3:17

Behold, I shew you a mystery; We shall not all sleep, but we shall all be changed.

In a moment, in the twinkling of an eye, at the last trump: for the trumpet shall sound, and the dead shall be raised incorruptible, and we shall be changed.

For this corruptible must put on incorruption, and this mortal *must* put on immortality.

So when this corruptible shall have put on incorruption, and this mortal shall have put on immortality, then shall be brought to pass the saying that is written, Death is swallowed up in victory.

O death, where *is* thy sting? O grave, where *is* thy victory?

The sting of death *is* sin; and the strength of sin *is* the law.

But thanks *be* to God, which giveth us the victory through our Lord Jesus Christ.

Therefore, my beloved brethren, be ye steadfast, unmoveable, always abounding in the work of the Lord, forasmuch as ye know that your labour is not in vain in the lord."
1 Corinthians 15:51-58

But as it is written, Eye hath not seen, nor ear heard, neither have entered into the heart of man, the things which God hath prepared for them that love him.
1 Corinthians 2:9

God loves all His creation and waits patiently for His bride because each human is precious to Him and God wants to bring as many as possible into the Body of Christ to share uncorruptible immortality. God created us in his image because He wants us with Him through eternity.

References

All Bible quotations are taken from the King James Bible KJV standard   https://www .kingjamesbibleonline.org/

The Church's Widowhood by Horatius Bonar, 1867 https://www.gracegems.org/Bonar /churchs_widowhood.htm

Watchmannee.org https://www.watchmannee .org/

Jewish Virtual Library https://www .jewishvirtuallibrary.org/, https://www .jewishvirtuallibrary.org/covering-of-the-head

Cover: https://biblehub.com/search .php?q=cover

Cover: https://www.biblegateway.com /quicksearch/?quicksearch=cover&version=NIV

Shaving of head: https://www.biblestudytools .com/dictionary/shaving/

Nazirite Vow: https://www.biblegateway.com/
quicksearch/?quicksearch=nazirite+vow
&version=NIV

About the Author

Cheryl Harris is not a professional writer or a Biblical scholar, but she has an investigative spirit and a love for the truth. Sitting down one day to read Ephesians and 1 Corinthians in the King James Bible she came across those hard to discern passages written by Paul discussing the Woman. An afternoon read evolved into two years of research and this little book. The real meaning of Paul's words is far mightier than the literal interpretation and is being presented for your Christian consideration.